Clutter Control

Tips and crafts to organize your bedroom, backpack, locker, life

★ AmericanGirl®

Published by American Girl Publishing, Inc.

Copyright © 2008 by American Girl, LLC

Questions or comments? Call 1-800-845-0005, visit our Web site at **americangirl.com**, or write to Customer Service, American Girl, 8400 Fairway Place, Middleton, WI 53562-0497.

Printed in China
11 12 13 14 15 16 LEO 10 9 8 7 6 5

Editorial Development: Erin Falligant, Jessica Hastreiter
Art Direction & Design: Chris Lorette David, Lara Klipsch Elliott
Production: Judith Lary, Mindy Rappe, Gretchen Krause, Jeannette Bailey
Stylists: Carrie Anton, Jessica Hastreiter; Illustrations: Tracy McGuinness

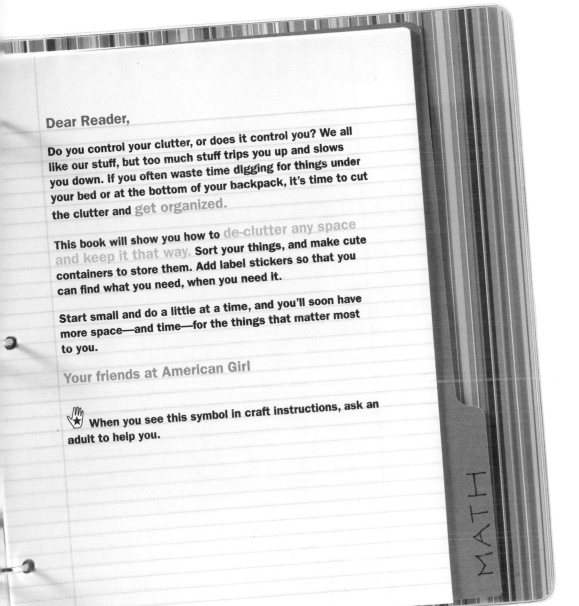

Dear Reader,

Do you control your clutter, or does it control you? We all like our stuff, but too much stuff trips you up and slows you down. If you often waste time digging for things under your bed or at the bottom of your backpack, it's time to cut the clutter and get organized.

This book will show you how to de-clutter any space and keep it that way. Sort your things, and make cute containers to store them. Add label stickers so that you can find what you need, when you need it.

Start small and do a little at a time, and you'll soon have more space—and time—for the things that matter most to you.

Your friends at American Girl

When you see this symbol in craft instructions, ask an adult to help you.

MATH

Uncluttered

Clutter Quiz . . . . .

Your Life . . . .

Your Backpack . .

Your Locker . . . . .

Your Bedroom . . .

Contents

7

9

15

23

35

Are You in Clutter Crisis?

Take a good hard look at your space and your stuff. Then check all the sentences that sound like you.

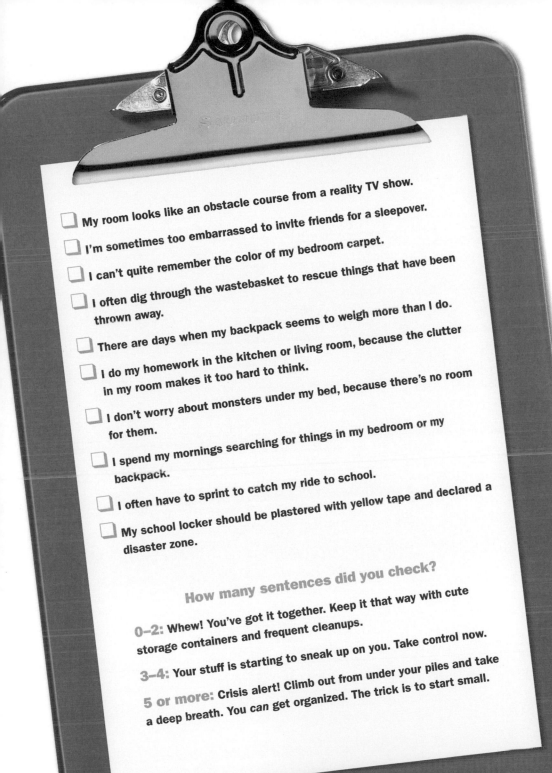

☐ My room looks like an obstacle course from a reality TV show.

☐ I'm sometimes too embarrassed to invite friends for a sleepover.

☐ I can't quite remember the color of my bedroom carpet.

☐ I often dig through the wastebasket to rescue things that have been thrown away.

☐ There are days when my backpack seems to weigh more than I do.

☐ I do my homework in the kitchen or living room, because the clutter in my room makes it too hard to think.

☐ I don't worry about monsters under my bed, because there's no room for them.

☐ I spend my mornings searching for things in my bedroom or my backpack.

☐ I often have to sprint to catch my ride to school.

☐ My school locker should be plastered with yellow tape and declared a disaster zone.

How many sentences did you check?

0–2: Whew! You've got it together. Keep it that way with cute storage containers and frequent cleanups.

3–4: Your stuff is starting to sneak up on you. Take control now.

5 or more: Crisis alert! Climb out from under your piles and take a deep breath. You *can* get organized. The trick is to start small.

Your Life

There are three basic steps to clutter control. Learn them, and you'll be able to organize any space—from your backpack to your bedroom. Ready to begin?

1
Sort It

Look at the stuff you have, and decide whether to keep it, toss it, or give it away.

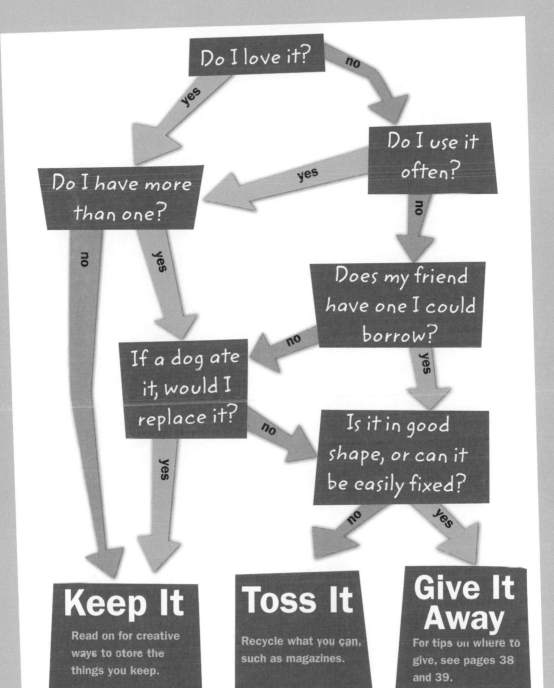

Do I love it?

yes

no

Do I use it often?

yes

no

Do I have more than one?

no

yes

Does my friend have one I could borrow?

no

yes

If a dog ate it, would I replace it?

yes

no

Is it in good shape, or can it be easily fixed?

no

yes

Keep It
Read on for creative ways to store the things you keep.

Toss It
Recycle what you can, such as magazines.

Give It Away
For tips on where to give, see pages 38 and 39.

2 Put It Away

After you decide what to keep, think about where to keep it. Everything needs a place so that you can find it when you need it.

Keep It Together

Barrettes should be with headbands, and pencils should be with pens. If you use things at the same time, such as your soccer ball and shin guards, store them together, too.

Box It, Bag It

Store your stuff in clear plastic bins so that you can see what's inside. Or reuse containers you already have, such as gift bags, baskets, and shoe boxes. Decorate the boxes with wrapping paper, and label the front of each box.

Put It Where You Use It

Hang your bag of hair accessories near your mirror. Slide your box of art supplies into a desk drawer. If you use something often, keep it out where you can grab it. If not, tuck it away in a drawer or on a shelf.

Keep It That Way!

It's much easier to stay organized than it is to get organized in the first place. Schedule a few minutes every day to put things away.

Your Backpack

Your clutter didn't appear all at once, and you don't have to get rid of it all at once. Start small—with your backpack.

Sort Your Pack

Can't find your homework beneath the heap of books and crumpled papers? Try this:

Empty everything out of your backpack. Everything.

Toss or recycle the trash. Get rid of the broken pencils, food wrappers, and invitations for parties that have come and gone.

Keep only those things that you'll use tonight or tomorrow:

- **the** worksheets, notebooks, and books that you need for today's homework. **The rest should stay in your locker.**

- **the** personal stuff that you'll need for tomorrow, **such as your flute or gym shoes.**

- tomorrow's lunch or lunch money.

- a few school supplies. **If you're toting 17 pencils, put most of them back into your desk or locker.**

Lighten Up

A too-heavy backpack can hurt your back, neck, and shoulders. What's too heavy? More than 10 percent of your body weight. If you weigh 80 pounds, your backpack should weigh no more than 8 pounds. Weigh your pack when it's full. If it's near the limit, lose the clutter and lighten up!

Repack It

There's not a lot of space in a backpack, so be smart about how you put things back in.

Take-Home Folder

Choose a folder with a bright color or bold pattern. Write "Take Me Home" on the front of the folder, and keep it in your backpack to hold loose worksheets and permission slips.

Pencil Pouch

Keep pencils, erasers, and other school supplies in a pencil pouch or plastic bag.

Cash and Keys

Do you have a zippered pocket on the front of your backpack? Store your small but important things inside—your lunch money, your house key, and a list of emergency phone numbers.

take me

Keep It Clutter-Free

You took the time to organize your backpack, so keep it that way. It takes just a few minutes a day.

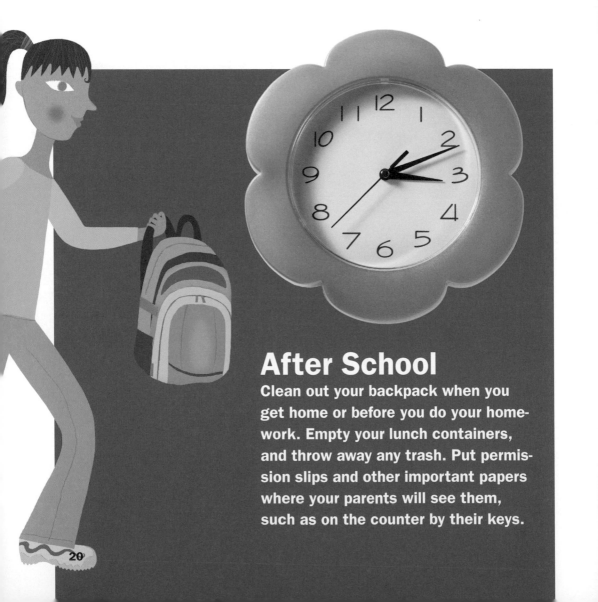

After School

Clean out your backpack when you get home or before you do your homework. Empty your lunch containers, and throw away any trash. Put permission slips and other important papers where your parents will see them, such as on the counter by their keys.

20

Before Bed

As soon as you finish your homework, put it in your backpack. Pack your lunch money, or pack a lunch and put it in the fridge. Do you need clothes for gym or sports practice? Signed permission slips or notes from your parents? Pack those, too.

In the Morning

What's left to do? Nothing! Just grab your backpack—and your lunch, if you made one—and go.

V.I.P. Pin
(Very Important Papers)

Need a place to put school papers for your parents to see and sign? Decorate a clothespin, and attach a magnet to the back. Stick the clothespin to the front of the refrigerator, where your parents will be sure to see it.

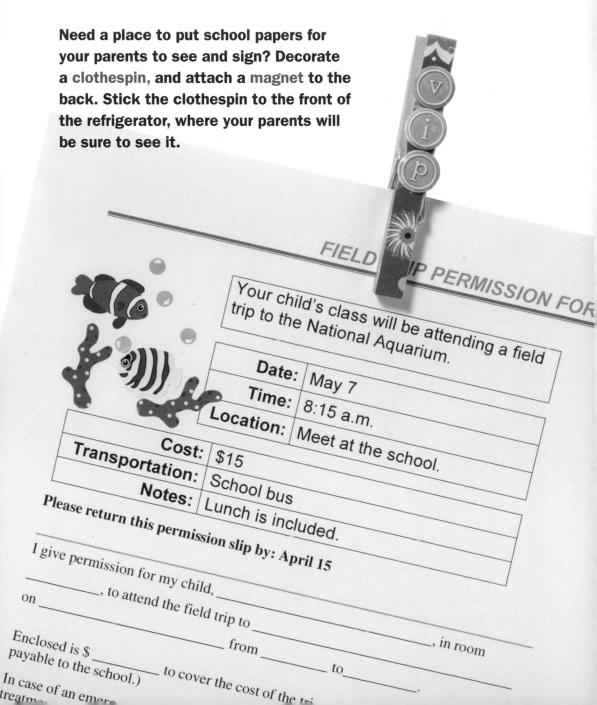

FIELD TRIP PERMISSION FOR

Your child's class will be attending a field trip to the National Aquarium.

Date:	May 7
Time:	8:15 a.m.
Location:	Meet at the school.
Cost:	$15
Transportation:	School bus
Notes:	Lunch is included.

Please return this permission slip by: April 15

I give permission for my child, _____,
_____, to attend the field trip to _____
on _____, in room
____. _____ from _____ to _____.
Enclosed is $ _____ to cover the cost of the trip.
payable to the school.)
In case of an emer
treatme

Your Locker

It's a fact—a messy locker slows you down. Cut the clutter to save time at school.

Lock It Up or Take It Home?

Before you sort the things in your locker, see what you know about what should stay and what should go.

1. Half of a granola bar still in the wrapper

2. Your dance outfit for next week's recital

3. The socks you wore in gym class today

4. Your piggy bank (the one you're hiding from your brother)

5. Your body spray, lip gloss, hair spray, and hand lotion

 l**ck it up**   **take it home** 🏠

6. The necklace your Aunt Marie gave you

 l**ck it up**   **take it home** 🏠

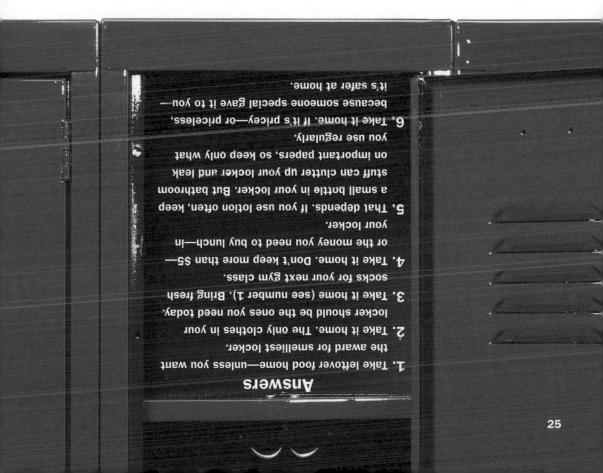

Answers

1. Take leftover food home—unless you want the award for smelliest locker.

2. Take it home. The only clothes in your locker should be the ones you need today.

3. Take it home (see number 1). Bring fresh socks for your next gym class.

4. Take it home. Don't keep more than $5—or the money you need to buy lunch—in your locker.

5. That depends. If you use lotion often, keep a small bottle in your locker. But bathroom stuff can clutter up your locker and leak on important papers, so keep only what you use regularly.

6. Take it home. If it's pricey—or priceless—because someone special gave it to you—it's safer at home.

Tame Paper Piles

Is your locker littered with crumpled notes, torn folders, and loose pieces of paper? Here's how to pick up the paper and sort it out.

Sort the Stacks

Toss or recycle old notes and announcements. Keep graded homework and quizzes, at least for a month. You may want them when you're studying for tests. Take home school papers that you don't think you'll need but that you still want to save.

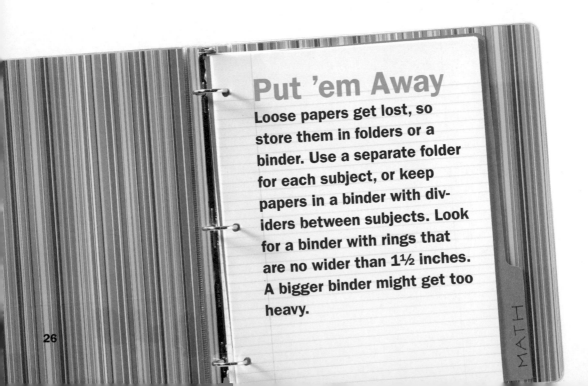

Put 'em Away

Loose papers get lost, so store them in folders or a binder. Use a separate folder for each subject, or keep papers in a binder with dividers between subjects. Look for a binder with rings that are no wider than 1½ inches. A bigger binder might get too heavy.

Play with Color

Color-code your things so that it's easy to grab what you need for each class. For science class, for example, use a green notebook, put handouts in a green folder, and wrap a green cover around your textbook.

Wrap It Up

To make a book cover, use wrapping paper with a funky design. Or use black paper and decorate it with stickers. For a quick fabric cover, wrap a bright bandanna around your book and use double-stick tape to hold the edges in place.

Get Personal

When it comes to storing personal stuff at school, less is more.

Keep It Simple

Start out with a brush or comb and a small mirror. Add a few emergency supplies, such as tissues, adhesive bandages, and safety pins. Beyond that, store only what you know you'll use every day.

Shelve It

Store your personal stuff in a colorful shower caddy or a small plastic crate that fits on the top shelf of your locker. Leave the bottom of your locker empty for big, bulky items, such as textbooks and binders.

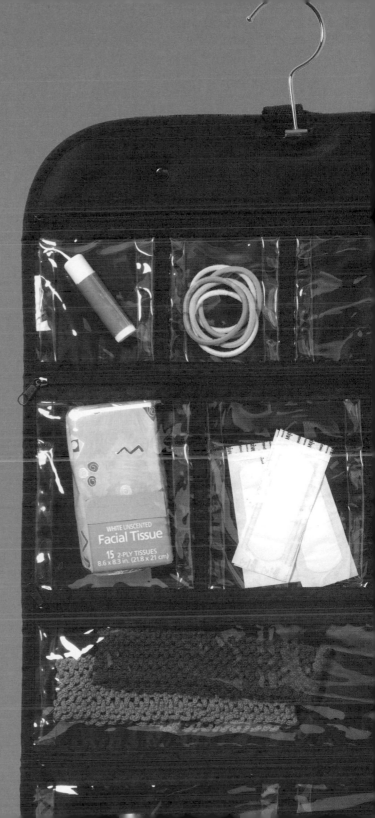

Hang It Up

For grab-and-go storage, use a traveling makeup kit. Slide your tissues and hair supplies into the clear plastic pockets, zip them up, and hang the kit from a magnetic hook.

Memos and Mementos

Want to hang on to the photos and notes that make your locker your own? Try hanging them up and out of the way on a locker-sized bulletin board.

Mini Memo Board

Start with a plain cork square, available at an office supply store. Cut a piece of fabric or felt that's the same size as the square. Glue the fabric to the square and let dry. Glue strong magnets to the back of the board (one in each corner), and let dry.

Fun-Tacks

Glue buttons, beads, silk flowers, rhinestones, or other scrapbooking embellishments to flat-backed tacks. Put a dot of glue on the head of the tack, and press the object to the tack for a few seconds. Let the tack dry head down.

Note: Check school rules before hanging anything in your locker.

Cool Tools

Look for other creative ways to keep your locker under control.

Hook

Stick a magnetic or adhesive hook on the inside of your locker door. Hang a pencil pouch or sweater from the hook.

Shelves or Drawers

Stack plastic shelves or drawers on the bottom of your locker. Organize your books on the shelves, or tuck school supplies into the drawers and stack your books on top.

Dry-Erase Board

Don't clutter your locker with reminder notes. Instead, hang up a dry-erase board for jotting down homework assignments and other important information.

Hanging Organizer

Look for a locker organizer that has pockets for your pencils and sticky notes. Some have built-in mirrors, too.

hook

locker shelf

hanging organizer

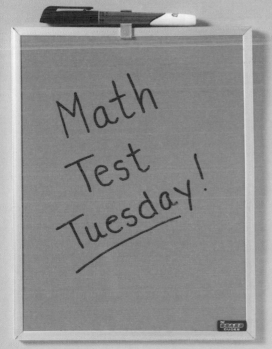

Math Test Tuesday!

dry-erase board

The Clean Routine

Keep your locker in tip-top shape with regular checkups.

Every Day

Pack your backpack after each class. If you have math homework, tuck your math book and notebook into your backpack before going to your next class. That'll keep your locker organized plus save you time at the end of the day.

Every Week

Pick one day of the week, say Friday, to clean out your locker. Take out every book, folder, and piece of paper. Put back in only the things that belong. Toss the trash, and take the rest home.

Your Bedroom

Organizing your room is not about being a neat freak. It's about knowing where things are so that you can find them and use them.

Start Smart

Don't try to sort your entire bedroom all at once. Start with some of these strategies. Which ones work best for you?

- **Make your bed and pick up your clothes. Those two steps will make your room look more organized and give you confidence to keep going.**

- **Tackle the biggest mess, or the clutter that's bothering you the most, first.**

- **Sort a small space, such as a desk drawer or the top of your dresser. Finish one small space before moving on to another.**

- **Set a timer if you're sorting a large space, such as your clothes closet. Try sorting for 15 minutes at a time.**

- **Carry a bag or basket as you make one clean sweep of your room. Collect things that are in the wrong spot or that don't have a place. Now sort those things before putting them away or finding them a home.**

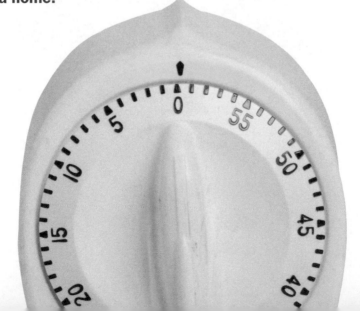

- As you sort a space, use boxes to separate the stuff. Label the boxes:

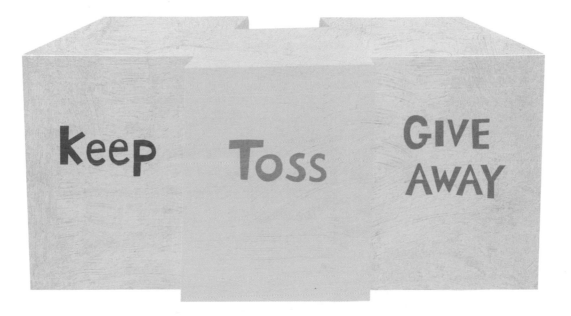

- Ask yourself the questions on page 11. They'll help you decide what stays and what goes.

Give It Away

As you change and grow, your interests do, too. Finding a good home for the things you've outgrown can make it easier to part with them.

- **Give books** to libraries, hospitals, and after-school programs in your community.

- **Give clothes and toys** to homeless shelters, Goodwill, the Salvation Army, and other community donation centers.

- **Give stuffed animals and dolls** to a younger relative or friend who you know will cherish them just as much as you did.

Or $ell It

Turn clutter into cash at thrift sales, resale stores, and online selling sites. Ask an adult to help you . . .

- sell computer games, CDs, and DVDs at resale music and movie stores.

- sell sports equipment at resale sporting-goods stores.

- sell collectibles online.

- sell just about anything at a family or neighborhood garage sale.

Try It

If you're struggling with giving something away, do an experiment. Ask an adult to put the item away for a few months to see if you really miss it. Or share it with a sibling or a friend so that you can still use it part of the time.

In the Zones

The best place to put things away in your room is wherever you'll use them most. Divide your room into zones—one area for each thing you do while you're there.

Homework Zone

This is your desk or wherever you do your schoolwork. You might have art supplies here, too.

Entertainment Zone

This is where you hang out when a friend comes over or when you just want to relax. Maybe you have a stereo, CDs, books, and games in this space.

Get-Ready Zone

Where do you get ready for school in the morning? Do you have a mirror in your room? This is the place to store jewelry and hair accessories.

Clothes Zone

Your clothes closet and dresser are part of this zone.

Think about your **sleep zone,** too—your bed. To make sure you get good sleep, try not to use your bed for other things, such as doing homework or piling laundry.

Homework Zone

To keep your desk free of clutter, know what to tuck away in drawers and what to leave out on top.

No-Mess Desktop

What stays out? Only those things you use every day, such as pencils, pens, and scissors. Store them in fun containers:

- glass jars **decorated with** hair elastics **or** rubber bands

- coffee mugs

- a teapot—**toss paper clips and erasers into a matching** teacup **or a pretty** dish **or** plate.

- a bottle **or** vase **wrapped in** chenille stems—**twist the ends of the chenille stems at the back of the bottle.**
  ✋⭐ **Have an adult help you carefully trim the ends with scissors.**

Magne-Tins

Need a place to store the small stuff? Clean out circular candy tins. **Decorate the lids with** paper, **and add** labels.

Project Stockpile

Use a box, **a** basket, **or an** under-the-bed bin **to store supplies you might need for school projects. Gather poster board, stickers, scrapbook paper, chenille stems, stencils, paint, ribbon, fabric scraps, and other supplies. If you keep them handy at home, you won't need to run out at the last minute to get them.**

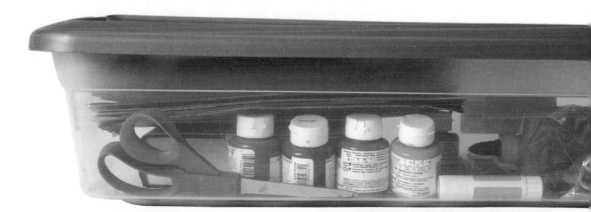

Paper Places

Don't litter in your homework zone. Store paper in creative places:

- **sideways in a** napkin holder

- **in a** canvas bag **tied to the back of your desk chair**

- **in** file folders **in a desk drawer or cardboard box. Label the folders with what's inside, such as "artwork," "homework," and "tests."**

- **in** frames **on your walls. Hang your favorite artwork where you can see it and be inspired by it.**

- **in a mailbox. Decorate the box with bright magnets. Put up the red flag when the box holds something special, such as a letter from a relative that you want to answer.**

- **in the trash.**

  Well, O.K., that's not a good place

  to store paper, but it's the place

  to put schoolwork from last grading period.

  If you want to hang on to reports or art

  projects, choose your favorite five.

  Throw away or recycle the rest.

Entertainment Zone

When your homework's done, you need a place to unwind. Make sure your fun stuff is easy to find—and to put away.

CDs

Slip your favorites into a metal letter rack or a colorful shower caddy.

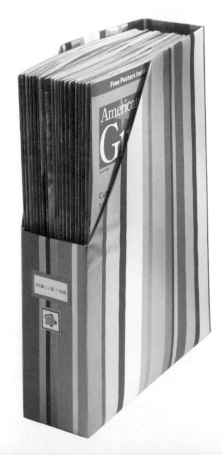

Magazines

Make a magazine holder out of an empty cereal box. Cut the box diagonally on both sides, and cover it with wrapping paper.

Books

If you don't have shelves, store your books in baskets or plastic crates. Or use bookends to prop up a few books on your nightstand.

Brick-Ends

Choose 2 bricks to use as bookends.  Have an adult help you spray-paint the bricks outdoors. Apply primer and 1 to 2 coats of paint, letting the paint dry in between coats. Decorate with stickers or felt shapes. To create patterns, paint the bricks with one color and press stickers to the bricks before painting with another color. (Peel the stickers off when the paint is dry.) Glue felt to the bottom of the bricks so that they won't scratch your furniture.

Get-Ready Zone

Tidy up a messy dresser with helpful hangers and cute containers.

Press It

Press a suction-cup soap holder against your mirror to store hair supplies right where you need them.

Contain It

Drop earrings, barrettes, and hair elastics into an ice-cube tray on your dresser.

Hang It

 Ask an adult to help you hang a coat rack on your wall. Dangle necklaces and bracelets from the hooks.

Clip It

Clip barrettes onto a ribbon that you hang on your wall. Cut a length of wide ribbon, and lay a narrow ribbon on top. Use binder clips to hold the ribbons together at the top and bottom.

Clothes, a Zone of Their Own

Looking for a way to organize your closet? Try these four fashionable ideas.

Arrange your closet . . .

- **by season.** Put last season's clothes at the back of the closet or in a bin under your bed.

- **by style.** Hang all of your short-sleeved shirts together, then your button-down shirts, and then your sweaters and long-sleeved tees. Keep pants with pants and skirts with skirts.

- **by color.** Keep reds and oranges at one end and blues and purples at the other. Mix and match outfits from the rainbow of colors.

- **by size.** Hang your long pants and skirts on one end and your shorter skirts and shirts at the other end. Tuck a shoe rack beneath your shorter clothes.

Stress-Free Dressing

Save time on weekday mornings by planning your outfits over the weekend. Hang a canvas clothing organizer in your closet. Label the shelves with the days of the week, using file folders that are trimmed to fit. Pick out outfits and place them on the shelves, along with any assignments or gear you'll need each day.

52

Shoe Solutions

Stack shoes on a shoe rack to keep them organized and to help prevent scuff marks. If you have a double rack, place boots or everyday shoes on the top rack within easy reach. No room for a rack? Try an over-the-door shoe organizer instead.

Basket Basics

Don't let your dirty clothes hit the floor.

Toss them into a hamper or laundry basket.

If you don't have one in your room,

talk to a parent about

getting one.

Your Special Things

What about photos, cards, stuffed animals, and souvenirs? They take up space in every zone, but they're hard to part with. Here's how to keep keepsakes from cluttering up your room:

friends

family

vacation

Store Them

Sort photos into photo boxes or shoe boxes wrapped in wrapping paper. (Remember to wrap lids separately!) Label the boxes "friends," "family," "vacations," "pets," and so on. If you think you'll forget the name of a person or place, write the name on the back of the photo (using an acid-free pen) before putting it into a box.

Scrap Them

Turn piles of loose photos and notes into scrapbooks that you'll want to page through again and again. Make a travel scrapbook of photos and souvenirs from a family trip. Or make a school scrapbook that holds friends' pictures and other school mementos.

Gather Them

Keep collections together. Do you have a ton of stuffed animals? Put your favorites into a big basket. Do you collect porcelain pigs? Arrange them together on a shelf. They'll look less cluttered and more special if they're all in one place.

Display Them

Turn your favorite photos and cards into dynamite displays:

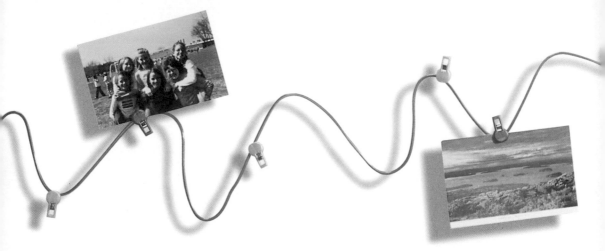

• 🖐 **Ask an adult to help you hang** plastic-coated electrical wire **across your wall. Bend the wire into a squiggly line, and make a small loop on each end to hang from a nail or a hook. Clip mementos to the wire to make a wall of memories.**

• **Tack mementos onto a** bulletin board **in a living collage—one that you re-arrange often. Replace some of the photos and notes every week. Otherwise, you'll get bored with your board and stop seeing what's on it.**

- **Cut patterned paper to fit the pockets of a plastic trading-card sleeve. Tape or glue school photos onto the pieces of paper, and slide them into the pockets. Punch two holes at the top of the sleeve, and use a ribbon to hang the pocket pictures.**

- ✋ **Ask an adult to help you find a sheet of acrylic plastic (found at home improvement stores) that fits the top of your desk or dresser. Tape a collage of photos to patterned paper, and arrange the paper on your desk or dresser top. Lay the plastic over the pictures for a pretty and practical display.**

Keep the Waste Away

What's your number one defense against clutter? A wastebasket. Dress yours up, and you'll be more likely to use it!

Pretty Paper

Cover portions of your basket with Mod Podge, using a sponge brush. Attach pieces of torn paper, overlapping the edges. Finish with another coat of Mod Podge, and let dry.

Fun Fur

Have an adult help you trim faux fur to fit around your basket. Attach the fur with tacky glue, and let dry. Finish with a ribbon.

Sweet Spots

Make a polka-dot pattern using sticky dots from an office supply store. Or punch circles out of card stock and glue on.

Bitty Beads

Cut beaded ribbon trim to fit the top of your basket. Use double-stick tape to attach the trim. Add adhesive gems.

Fluffy Stuff

Trim a feather boa to fit the top of your basket. Attach the boa with binder clips, and add silk flowers with tacky glue.

Keep It Clean, Keep It Fun

Set aside a few minutes every day to put your things away.

Pick a Time

Choose a few minutes **in the morning, after school, or before bed. Make a habit out of picking up your room at the same time every day. Eventually, you won't have to think about it—you'll just do it. That means you'll have less to do at the end of the week, and you'll have a clean, clutter-free room every day.**

Be Creative

Routine room cleanups don't have to be boring. Make them fun, and they'll be easier to stick with. Try this:

- Set an egg timer for 15 minutes. Challenge yourself to put everything in its place before the timer dings.

- Pretend that your room is a fancy boutique. Arrange everything nicely so that your customers will want to come back.

- Play hoops with your dirty laundry or crumpled notepaper. Where do you have to stand in your room to make a 3-point shot?

- Imagine that you're hosting a home improvement show. Describe to your audience what you're doing and why.

BIG
Truth

The time you spend clearing out the clutter will save you oodles of time later on. That means more time for the important stuff—homework, friends, family, and fun. Be smart about how you fill your space *and* your time.

How do you control your clutter? Which tips and crafts worked best for you?

Write to:
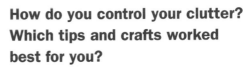
Clutter Control Editor
American Girl
8400 Fairway Place
Middleton, WI 53562

(All comments and suggestions received by American Girl may be used without compensation or acknowledgment. Sorry—photos can't be returned.)

Here are some other American Girl books you might like:

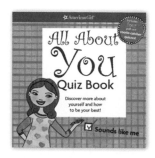

❏ I read it.

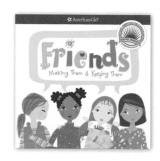

❏ I read it.

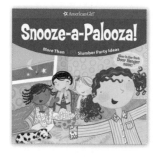

❏ I read it.

❏ I read it.

❏ I read it.

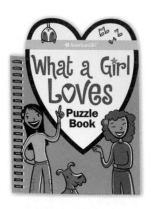

❏ I read it.

rubber bands	tacks	paper clips	hair things	odds & ends	candy tin labels

artwork

homework

tests

notes & letters

photos

photos

friends

family

vacation

pets

my
music

jewelry

odds &
ends

hair
things

magazines

important

notes &
letters

craft
stuff

school
stuff

keep-
sakes

don't
peek

keep
out

take me
home

a a a
b b c
c d d
e e e

f f g g h h i i i j j
k k l l m m n n o o
o p p q q r r r s s s
t t t u u v v w w x x
y y z z 1 2 3 4 5 6 7
8 9 0 ! ! ! . . ? ? ?